Steck-

MW01269089

Language Handbook

Level B

First Steck-Vaughn Edition 1999

Copyright © by Harcourt Brace & Company

Printed in the United States of America

ISBN 0-8172-8602-0

1 2 3 4 5 6 7 8 9 02 01 00 99 98

STECK-VAUGHN
C O M P A N Y

A Division of Harcourt Brace & Company

Contents

TABLE OF CONTENTS

HANDWRITING

ADDITIONAL PRACTICE

Dear Student,

Every time you listen to a story, or talk to someone, or watch a show, you're using language. Whenever you write a message, do homework, or make a book, you're using language, too. You already know a lot about how your language works! But there's more to learn about spoken and written English. We hope you enjoy using what you find out.

Sincerely,

The Authors

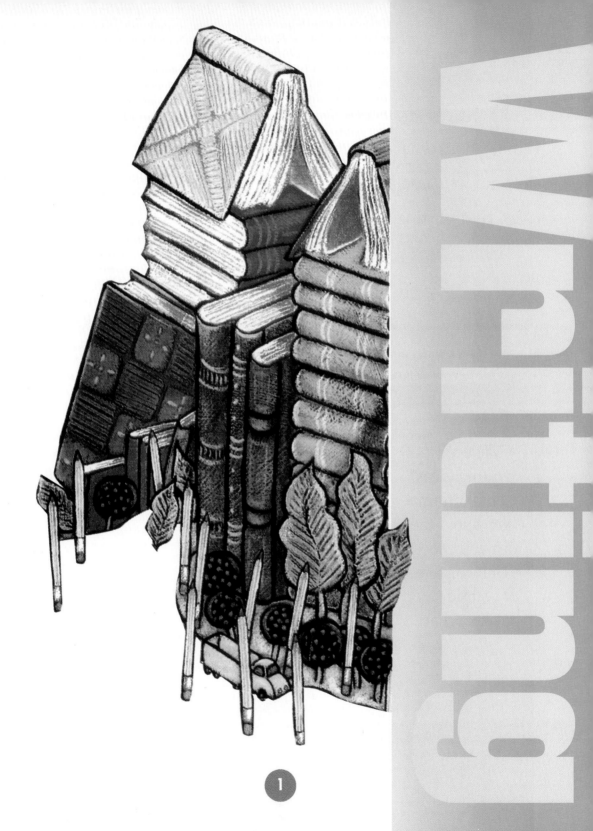

1

The Writing Process

When you write a story or a poem, a plan can help you. Think about <u>what</u> you want to write, <u>who</u> you are writing for, and <u>why</u> you are writing. Then, use these five stages to plan your writing.

PREWRITING

- Make a list of writing ideas.
- Find information about the idea you choose.
- Draw a picture of your idea, or make a chart.

DRAFTING

Write about your prewriting idea, or change your idea. Do not worry about mistakes.

RESPONDING AND REVISING

Meet with a partner to talk about your draft.

PROOFREADING

Use your handbook to talk with a partner to correct your writing.

PUBLISHING

Decide how you want to publish your work.

3

THE WRITING PROCESS

Personal Journal

A **personal journal** is a place where you can write down your thoughts or important ideas. Writing in your journal helps you keep a record of interesting things that happen.

- **Write the date.**

- **Write about interesting things that happened.**

- **Tell why these things are important to you.**

MODEL: PERSONAL JOURNAL

date	September 2, 199—
what happened	Today was my first piano lesson. I was so nervous. But
why it is important	I loved playing! The half hour flew by. My teacher said I did a great job!

Paragraph

A **paragraph** is a group of sentences that tell about one main idea. A paragraph begins with a topic sentence. The **topic sentence** tells the main idea. The other sentences are called detail sentences. **Detail sentences** tell about the main idea.

- Write a topic sentence that tells the main idea of your paragraph.

- Indent the first line.

- Write detail sentences that tell about the main idea.

M O D E L : P A R A G R A P H

topic sentence

detail sentences

I like going to the fair. The roller coaster is my favorite ride. I was scared the first time I rode it. Now I think it is a lot of fun. I also like playing the games and winning prizes.

Personal Story

In a **personal story**, a writer tells about something that has happened in his or her life. A personal story can tell how the writer feels about something. It has words like I, me, and my.

- **Think of things that have happened in your life. Choose one to tell about.**

- **Write your story in the order in which things happened. Use time-order words like first, next, then, and last.**

- **Use words like I and me to tell about yourself.**

It was the last inning. We were behind by one run. There were two outs, and then I was at bat.

I swung at the first pitch and missed. Strike one! Then I hit a foul ball. Strike two! On the next pitch, I kept my eye on the ball. I hit the ball hard and started to run. At first, I didn't hear the cheers. Then I knew. Finally, I had hit my first home run!

Time-order words help show the order in which things happen.

Story

A **story** tells about real or make-believe events.
A story has a beginning, a middle, and an ending.

- Write a beginning. Tell who the characters are, where the story takes place, and what the problem is.

- Write the middle. Tell what happens to the characters. Tell what they do.

- Write the ending. Tell how the problem is solved.

- Write a title for your story.

title

beginning

middle

ending

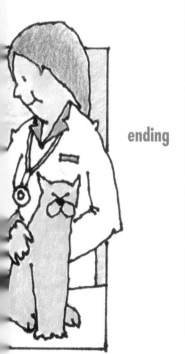

Junior Vet

 I think I might want to be a veterinarian someday. So I asked Dr. Curry if I could help her out for a week. Dr. Curry let me feed the animals and watch her work. At the end of the week, she asked if I still wanted to be an animal doctor. "More than ever," I answered. I meant every word!

Sentences About a Picture

A **sentence** tells a complete thought. It begins with a capital letter. It ends with an end mark.

- Choose an idea.

- Draw a picture that shows your idea.

- Write a sentence that tells the main idea of your picture.

- Be sure your sentence tells a complete thought.

capital letter

end mark

Dad likes to paint the flowers in the garden.

Friendly Letter

In a **friendly letter**, a writer writes to someone he or she knows. A friendly letter has five parts.

- Write your address and the date as the heading.

- Write a greeting to say hello.

- Write a friendly message in the body.

- Write a closing to end your letter.

- Sign your name under the closing.

heading

24 Tampa Way
Ocala, Florida 32670
October 23, 199—

greeting

Dear Kate,

body

I'm finally getting used to my new school. At first, it was hard. The school is so big, and I didn't know anyone. Now I know my way around. I am making new friends, too. I still miss my old friends, though. Please write!

closing

Your friend,

signature

LaTisha

Invitation

In an **invitation**, a writer invites someone to come somewhere or to do something. An invitation has five parts.

- Write the date as the heading.

- Write a greeting to say hello.

- Write the body. Tell who is invited. Tell what the invitation is for. Tell when and where the event will take place.

- Write a closing to end your invitation.

- Sign your name under the closing.

heading

March 23, 199

greeting

Dear Mitch,

body

I am having a party so my friends can meet my new neighbor, Theo. It will be on April 1 at 3:00 P.M. at my house. I live at 408 Walter Road. Please let me know if you can come.

closing

signature

Your pal,
Jasmine

Thank-you Note

In a **thank-you note**, a writer thanks someone for something. You can write a thank-you note for a gift. You can write a thank-you note for something nice someone did. A thank-you note has five parts.

MODEL: THANK-YOU NOTE

heading

April 3, 199—

greeting

Dear Jasmine,

body

    Thank you for inviting me to your party. I really had fun. I liked meeting Theo, too. Maybe he will join our team this summer.

closing

Your friend,

signature

Mitch

Envelope

An **envelope** is used to send a letter.

The **return address** names the person who is sending the letter.

The **mailing address** names the person who will get the letter.

MODEL: ENVELOPE

return address

Kayla Wicker
162 Magnolia Street
Pomona, California 93944

mailing address

Sharon Johnson
2909 Buck Run Drive
Richmond, Virginia 23261

Paragraph That Describes

In a **paragraph that describes**, a writer describes a person, an animal, a place, or a thing. The writer uses describing words that help the reader see, hear, taste, smell, and feel.

- Write a topic sentence to tell who or what your paragraph is about.

- Write sentences that tell what the person, animal, place, or thing is like.

- Use words that give a good word picture.

me →

topic sentence

describing words in detail sentences

My family went to visit Mammoth Cave in Kentucky. It is a very big cave. It is cold and dark on the inside. When the lights are turned off, you can't even see your hands! The walls are wet and feel slimy. The whole cave has a damp smell.

Poem

In a **poem**, a writer describes something in an interesting way. Some poems have rhyming words. These poems often have a **rhythm**, or **beat**, that makes them fun to read.

Other poems do not rhyme. These poems "paint" word pictures with colorful words.

- **Paint a good word picture.**
- **Use rhyming words if you want to.**
- **Give your poem a title.**

title

rhyme

New Neighbor
The moving van is here.
And what is that I see?
A bike that's just like mine,
And one new friend for me!

title

no rhyme

Night Sounds
The train rumbles and horns
    honk.
Footsteps pass my window.
Voices shout hello.
These are the night sounds
    in my neighborhood.

Paragraph That Gives Information

In a **paragraph that gives information**, a writer gives facts and details about one topic.

- Write a topic sentence. Tell who or what your paragraph is about.

- Indent the first line.

- Write detail sentences. Give interesting facts about the person, animal, place, or thing.

topic sentence

detail sentences

    Many African American people celebrate Kwanzaa. It is a celebration of the customs and history of African American people. It is a gathering time for families, like Thanksgiving.

    The holiday is celebrated for seven days. It begins the day after Christmas. On each night of Kwanzaa, a candle is lit. Each candle stands for a rule to help people live their lives.

Book Report

A **book report** tells what a book is about. It names the title, the author, and the illustrator of the book. It also tells what someone thinks about the book.

- Write the title of the book.

- Write the author's name. Write the illustrator's name, if there is one.

- Write sentences that tell what the book is about. Tell about important people, places, and things.

- Write what you think about the book. Tell why you like or do not like the book.

title	<u>The Popcorn Dragon</u>
author	Jane Thayer
illustrator	Lisa McCue
What the book is about	A dragon named Dexter liked to blow smoke. He wanted to have friends. The other animals didn't like him because he was always showing off. Then Dexter discovered he could use his hot breath to make something special.

Play

In a **play**, an author writes a story to act out.
People play the parts of the characters in the story.

- **Think of a story to tell.**

- **Decide what characters are in the story.**

- **Decide when and where the story takes place.**

- **Write what the characters say.**

- **Write what the characters do.**

characters

when

where

what characters
say

what characters
do

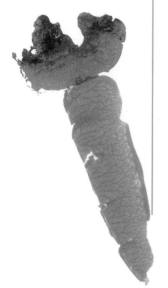

CHARACTERS: MOTHER, GWEN, BANTA (a rabbit)

TIME: morning

SETTING: a garden

MOTHER: Gwen, I'm going to the office. While I'm gone, please plant the garden.

GWEN: Yes, Mother.

(Mother leaves.)

BANTA: Come play with me?

GWEN: Who said that?

BANTA: I did.

How-to Paragraph

In a **how-to paragraph**, a writer gives directions that tell how to make or do something. The steps are in order.

- Write a sentence to name your topic.

- Write a sentence that tells what things are needed. This is the first step.

- Write steps in the correct order to tell how to make or do something.

- Use the words first, next, then, and last to show the order of the steps.

First

Next

topic sentence

things that are needed

steps

Did you know that you can water your plants even when you're not home? You'll need thin cotton rope and a glass of water. First, put the glass of water next to your plant. Next, push one end of the rope into the soil. Last, put the other end of the rope in the water. The water will travel through the rope from the glass to the plant.

Last

Research Report

To write a **research report**, a writer gathers information from different books and magazines and takes **notes**. Then he or she uses the notes to tell about the topic.

- Take notes about your topic.

- Use your notes to write a few paragraphs about your topic.

- Give your research report a title.

title

main topic

facts

Busy As a Bee

There are three kinds of honeybees. The queen bee is the biggest. Her job is to lay eggs in the nest. Male bees are the drones. It is their job to help the queen. The smallest bees are the worker bees. Worker bees collect nectar from flowers and bring it back to the nest. Other worker bees make honey from the nectar.

Poster That Persuades

In a **poster that persuades**, a writer shows a problem. He or she draws a picture and writes words to show how the problem could be solved.

- Decide on a topic. What is the problem? How could it be solved?

- Draw a picture.

- Write your ideas about the picture. Use some catchy words.

33

Writing for a Test

When you take a **writing test**, be sure you understand what to do. Read <u>all</u> the directions.

Imagine that this cat comes to your house. Think about its size and color. Think about what you would name it. Write a paragraph about the cat.

A new cat came to our house. She is a girl cat. She is really big and fat like a dog. Her fur is yellow with brown stripes. Her nose is soft and pink. I named her Daizee.

SENTENCES

A **sentence** is a group of words that tells a complete thought. Every sentence begins with a capital letter and ends with a special mark.

sentence

My friend rides a bike.

not a sentence

my friend

Exercises

A. Read each group of words. Tell if the words make a sentence.

1. My birthday present was a bike.
2. blue and white bike
3. I tried to ride it.
4. fell down
5. Dad helped me learn.

B. Write the groups of words that are sentences.

1. My dog's name is Max.
2. Max likes to jump.
3. my smart dog
4. lots of tricks
5. I laugh a lot with Max.
6. Max works hard.
7. can roll over
8. My dog and I are friends.
9. give Max treats
10. Max and the cat

For additional practice, turn to page 116.

NAMING PART

A sentence has a **naming part** that names who or
what the sentence is about.

Grandmother has a garden.

Red roses bloom in the garden.

The roses smell sweet.

Exercises

A. Find the naming part in each sentence.

1. Grandmother likes to grow flowers.
2. Melanie helps her grandmother.
3. They plant seeds in the soil.
4. Water helps the plants grow.
5. The plants grow tall.
6. Grandfather pulls the weeds.
7. The flowers are different colors.

B. Choose a naming part from the box to begin each sentence. Then write the sentence.

Green peas　**Strawberries**
Orange pumpkins　**The garden**
This tomato　**The farmer**

1. _____ has a garden.
2. _____ has lots of vegetables.
3. _____ grow in pods.
4. _____ grow slowly.
5. _____ need water.
6. _____ is too green to eat.

For additional practice, turn to page 117.

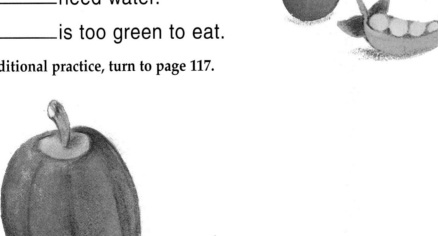

Joining Naming Parts

Sometimes the naming parts of two sentences can be joined. The word and is used to join the naming parts.

Bob came early.

Lin came early.

Bob and Lin came early.

Exercises

A. Join the naming parts of each pair of sentences. The naming parts are written in dark type. Use the word and.

1. **The children** were at the pool.
   The parents were at the pool.

2. **Nan** saw the swimming teacher.
   Jamal saw the swimming teacher.

3. **Anna** sat by the pool.
   Otto sat by the pool.

B. Complete the sentences by joining naming parts.
Write the sentences.

1. Nan jumped into the pool.
    Bob jumped into the pool.
    _____ and _____ jumped into the pool.

2. Mom watched us float.
    Dad watched us float.
    _____ and _____ watched us float.

3. Hannah paddled to the other side.
    Her friend paddled to the other side.
    _____ and _____ paddled to the other side.

For additional practice, turn to page 118.

GRAMMAR

Telling Part of a Sentence

TELLING PART

A sentence has a **telling part** that tells what someone or something <u>is</u> or <u>does</u>.

Marie <u>went fishing</u>.

She <u>caught a striped fish</u>.

Mom and Dad <u>cheered</u>.

Exercises

A. Find the telling part in each sentence.

1. We drove to the lake.
2. Dad put bait on the hook.
3. The worm wiggled.
4. Mom caught two fish.
5. A fish pulled on my line.
6. I caught a big fish!
7. We ate fish for supper.

B. Look at the picture. Use the words in the box to add a telling part to each sentence. Write the sentence.

starts the fire	**sleeps under a tree**
watches us	**fixes the tent**

1. Dad _____.

2. Mom _____.

3. A squirrel _____.

4. The dog _____.

For additional practice, turn to page 119.

JOINING TELLING PARTS

Sometimes the telling parts of two sentences can be joined. The word <u>and</u> is used to join the telling parts.

Shana eats fruit.

Shana drinks milk.

Shana eats fruit <u>and</u> drinks milk.

44

Exercise

Join the telling parts of each pair of sentences. Use the word <u>and</u>.

1. Shana rides a bike.
   Shana wears a helmet.

2. She brushes her teeth.
   She washes her face.

3. Shana walks with Buddy.
   Shana crosses at the light.

4. Buddy does tricks.
   Buddy chases balls.

5. Buddy sleeps all day.
   Buddy waits for Shana after school.

For additional practice, turn to page 120.

Word Order

WORD ORDER

The words in a sentence are in an order that makes sense. If the words are mixed up, the sentence does not make sense.

sentence

Karen likes to play basketball.

not a sentence

basketball play Karen likes to.

Exercises

A. Read each group of words. Tell if the order of the words makes sense.

1. Karen has a favorite game.
2. game The is basketball.
3. friends meets after school She.
4. They play until dinnertime.

B. Write each group of words in the correct order.

1. Abdul Florida in lives.
2. collects seashells He.
3. helps him His brother.
4. find They shells pretty.
5. shells are Some all white.
6. the shells carry They home.
7. makes from Abdul shells things.
8. them on cans He glues.
9. The pencils cans hold.
10. the Abdul pencil holders sells.

For additional practice, turn to page 121.

GRAMMAR

Statements

STATEMENT

A **statement** is a sentence that tells something. It ends with a **period** (.).

Now Turtle and Frog are friends.

Exercises

A. Tell how you would write each statement correctly.

1. there are many friends for Turtle
2. he plays on Frog's swing set
3. they take the bus to school together
4. at school they play with Rabbit
5. their favorite game is tag
6. it's easy to catch Turtle
7. one of Turtle's favorite games is hide-and-seek
8. he just hides in his shell

B. Read each sentence. Find statements that have mistakes. Write those statements correctly.

1. the friends see Snake and Rat.
2. Snake and Rat are in fourth grade.
3. All the animals are afraid of them
4. today Turtle plays a trick on Rat
5. he asks Rabbit and Frog to help
6. together they plan what they will do.
7. First they go behind the slide.

C. Write three statements. Tell how Turtle and his friends play a trick on Snake and Rat. Use capital letters and periods.

For additional practice, turn to page 122.

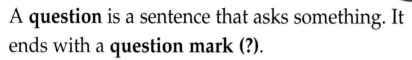

QUESTION

A **question** is a sentence that asks something. It ends with a **question mark (?)**.

What time is it?

Exercises

A. Read each sentence. Decide if it is a question. If it is, tell how you would write it correctly.

1. where are you going

2. now I'm going to the park

3. are you going alone

4. there I will meet my friend Beth

5. she is bringing her cousin

6. do you know her cousin

7. she will be a new friend

B. Begin each sentence with a question word from the box. Write the question. Use the correct end mark.

How	Who	Will
Where	What	When

1. _____is your name

2. _____old are you

3. _____do you start school

4. _____walks to school with you

5. _____is your classroom

6. _____you be my friend

For additional practice, turn to page 123.

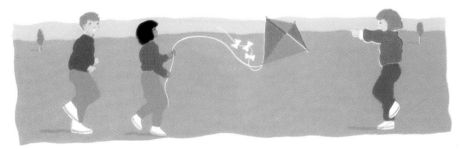

Exclamations and Commands

EXCLAMATION

An **exclamation** is a sentence that shows strong feeling. It ends with an **exclamation point (!)**.

What fun it is to make new friends!

COMMAND

A **command** is a sentence that tells someone to do something. It ends with a **period (.)**.

Throw the ball to my friend.

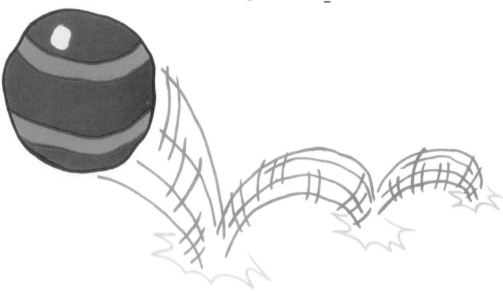

Exercises

A. Tell if each sentence is an exclamation or a command. Tell which end mark should be added.

1. Meet my new friends
2. What fun we are having today
3. Run before I catch you
4. Hooray for friends
5. Jump as high as you can
6. How fast the time went by

B. Finish the sentences. Write exclamations and commands. Use the correct end mark.

1. _____over here
2. How happy _____
3. _____tomorrow

For additional practice, turn to page 124.

PERIOD

A statement tells something. It ends with a **period (.)**.

I ride to school with my friends.

A command tells someone to do something. It also ends with a **period (.)**.

Meet me at the bus stop.

QUESTION MARK

A question asks something. It ends with a **question mark (?)**.

When will the bus come?

EXCLAMATION POINT

An exclamation shows strong feeling. It ends with an **exclamation point (!)**.

Here it is! Hurry up!

Exercises

A. Write each sentence correctly.

1. Do you have a special friend
2. My best friend had a party
3. What a surprise
4. We had cake
5. Pour more tea, please
6. Wow, these are yummy cookies
7. What did you talk about
8. Don't tell the secret
9. May I go next time
10. Hooray for surprise parties

B. Write four sentences. Tell about an animal party. Use each end mark at least once.

For additional practice, turn to page 125.

55

GRAMMAR

Nouns

PEOPLE

A word that names a person is called a **noun.**

The girl is ready.

ANIMALS

A word that names an animal is called a **noun.**

The dog wants to play, too.

PLACES

A word that names a place is called a **noun.**

It tries to run onto the field.

THINGS

A word that names a thing is called a **noun.**

The fence is too high.

Exercise

Read each sentence. Tell if the underlined noun names a person, an animal, a place, or a thing.

1. I like to play with my friends.
2. Today we are at the ballpark.
3. The pitcher gets ready to throw.
4. When she does, I swing my bat.
5. I hit the ball hard.
6. It sails over the players.
7. I hope it doesn't frighten the birds!
8. The fans cheer loudly.
9. We win the game!
10. Later we all buy ice cream at the store.

For additional practice, turn to page 126.

Special Names and Titles of People

NAMES OF PEOPLE

Some nouns are the names of people. These nouns are called **proper nouns.** Names of people begin with a capital letter.

Patricia Seanne is a writer.

TITLES OF PEOPLE

Titles of people also begin with a capital letter. Most titles are followed by a **period (.)**

Mrs. Costgrove is our teacher.

Exercises

A. Tell how you would write each sentence correctly.

1. My name is ruby walker.
2. My best friend is mrs anna gomez.
3. She and I visit dr randall.
4. His nurse, mr day, tells funny stories.

B. Look at the picture. Write a name for each person in the picture. Be sure to include a title for each person.

For additional practice, turn to page 127.

Names of Special Animals and Places

SPECIAL ANIMALS

Some **proper nouns** are the names of special animals. Names of special animals begin with capital letters.

> **My cat's name is <u>Slate</u>.**

SPECIAL PLACES

Some **proper nouns** are the names of special places. Names of special places begin with capital letters.

> **The vet's office is in <u>Milwaukee</u>.**

Exercises

A. Tell where you would add capital letters in each sentence.

1. We found our cat in new york.
2. We decided to name her liberty.

B. Complete each sentence with a proper noun.

1. The street I live on is _____.
2. I live in _____.
3. It is in the state of _____.
4. If I had a new pet, I would name it _____.

For additional practice, turn to page 128.

Names of Days and Months

DAYS

The names of days are **proper nouns.** The names of days begin with capital letters.

My birthday is this Sunday.

MONTHS

The names of months are **proper nouns.** The names of months begin with capital letters.

Spring begins in March.

Exercises

A. Tell how you would write each sentence correctly.

1. The wolf moved in september.
2. On monday, the little pig took him a cake.
3. The wolf called on tuesday for lunch.
4. The pig said she was busy until october.

B. Read each sentence. Write the name of a day or a month that is written correctly.

1. The pink pig said she would come to dinner on (monday, Monday).

2. On (wednesday, Wednesday), the wolf bought a big black pot for luck.

3. The pig bought some very large scissors in (December, december).

4. The pig went to the wolf's house on the tenth of (january, January).

5. In (February, february), the pig wore a new fur hat.

HOLIDAYS

The names of holidays are **proper nouns**. All important words in the names of holidays begin with capital letters.

We have a picnic on <u>Memorial Day</u>.

Exercises

A. Tell where you would add capital letters in each sentence.

1. Our town has fireworks on the fourth of july.
2. We go to a block party on labor day.
3. My class puts on a play on columbus day.
4. Mr. Simms cooks on thanksgiving day.
5. My family goes to New York City on new year's day.

B. Read each sentence. Write the name of the holiday that is written correctly.

1. On (arbor day, Arbor Day), we plant a tree.
2. We celebrate the Mexican holiday (Cinco de Mayo, cinco de mayo).
3. A holiday in spring is (May Day, may day).
4. Canada has (thanksgiving day, Thanksgiving Day) in October.
5. We celebrate (Earth Day, earth day) in March.
6. Did you play a trick on (April Fool's Day, april fool's day)?
7. We tell stories in our family for (kwanzaa, Kwanzaa).

For additional practice, turn to pages 129–130.

TITLES OF BOOKS

The first word, the last word, and each important word in a title begin with capital letters. The titles of books have a line under them.

Let's read The Friendly Dinosaur.

She wrote the book Will I Have a Friend?

Exercises

A. Tell where you would add capital letters in each sentence.

1. Have you read the book the long walk?
2. Last year, we read first grade takes a test.
3. This year, we read second grade friends.
4. My brother read the book how to survive third grade.
5. I want to read rent a third grader.

B. Write each book title correctly.

1. frog and toad together
2. froggy gets dressed
3. amazing frogs and toads
4. helpful snakes
5. turtles and other reptiles
6. never kiss a crocodile

C. Read each story idea. Make up a book title for each story. Write the title.

1. a grouchy neighbor
2. two neighbors who become friends
3. a funny story about your neighbor upstairs
4. a city lemonade stand

For additional practice, turn to page 131.

PLURAL NOUNS WITH <u>S</u>

Some nouns name more than one. Add the letter <u>s</u>
to most nouns to name more than one.

tree — trees   road — roads

Exercises

A. Read each sentence. Find the noun that names
more than one.

1. My family rode in two jeeps.
2. Each jeep had seats in the front and in the back.
3. We went on a ride with some friends.
4. We saw a mother lion and her two cubs.
5. Some monkeys were sitting in a tree.
6. Many elephants were standing by the fence.

B. Choose the correct noun. Write the sentence.

1. We saw only one (spaceship, spaceships).
2. The spaceship had many (light, lights).
3. They were all around the one (rim, rims).
4. They sparkled like many (jewel, jewels).
5. The spaceship looked like a (crown, crowns).
6. Then it disappeared behind a (cloud, clouds).
7. I've had many (dream, dreams) like that.

P L U R A L   N O U N S   W I T H   <u>E S</u>

Some nouns end with <u>es</u> to name more than one.

ditch — ditch<u>es</u>   **bench — bench<u>es</u>**

glass — glass<u>es</u>   **box — box<u>es</u>**

Exercises

A. Find the nouns that name more than one. They are spelled incorrectly. Spell them correctly.

1. Four class from our school went to the woods.
2. Did you see two baby fox?
3. They were playing under a bush.
4. Then we heard some crash of thunder.
5. Soon we saw a flash of lightning.
6. We ran fast to our two bus!
7. Both fox ran away.
8. I looked at my watch as we left.

B. Choose a noun from the box to complete each sentence. Make the noun mean more than one. Write the sentence.

sandwich bush peach bunch lunch

1. We are going to have two picnic _____.
2. Will you make chicken _____?
3. Here are some fresh _____, too.
4. Let's put our blanket between two _____.
5. Tory brought two _____ of grapes.

Other Plural Nouns

OTHER PLURAL NOUNS

Some nouns change spelling to name more than one.

man — men   woman — women

child — children   tooth — teeth

foot — feet

Exercises

A. Choose the correct noun.

1. One (woman, women) is working.
2. Many (men, man) are on horses.
3. A (child, children) is wading in the stream.
4. He has no shoes on his (feet, foot).
5. The cold water makes his (teeth, tooth) chatter.

B. Change the word in ( ) so that it names more than one. Write the sentences.

1. The (man) hunted buffalo.
2. The (woman) made buffalo robes.
3. They chewed the hide with their (tooth) to make it soft.
4. They made soft shoes for their (foot).
5. The (child) had new shirts.

For additional practice, turn to pages 132–133.

GRAMMAR

PRONOUNS

A **pronoun** is a word that takes the place of a noun. I, he, she, they, and it are pronouns.

I tells about the speaker. He and she tell about other people.

It tells about an animal or a thing. They tells about more than one.

At night he wakes up.

Exercise

Read the sentences. Think of a pronoun for the underlined words.

1. Janie and I sat on the back porch.
2. Did you see a raccoon by the garage?
3. My dad went to the garage.
4. My dad chased the raccoon away.

For additional practice, turn to page 134.

Kids on Language

My name is Margarita Nuesheva. I was born in Odessa, Ukraine. I can read and write in two alphabets! The Russian alphabet has many letters that look the same as the letters in the English alphabet, like *A*, *B*, and *H*. But they stand for different sounds. Now I mostly read and write in English and speak Russian at home. I help my mom understand TV shows when we watch them together.

75

GRAMMAR

DESCRIBING WORDS

A **describing word** tells about a noun.

TOUCH

Some describing words tell how something feels.

The animal was <u>soft</u>.

TASTE OR SMELL

Some describing words tell how something tastes
or smells.

I gave it a <u>sour</u> apple.

SOUND

Some describing words tell how something sounds.

Its <u>loud</u> cry scared me.

Exercises

A. Write the describing word in each sentence.

1. We sat on a bumpy log.
2. The hot fire glowed.
3. Can you hear the chirping crickets?
4. The fire made loud noises.
5. The marshmallows were sweet.
6. What is that smoky smell?
7. My apple is crunchy.

B. Write three sentences about your favorite fruit. Tell how it feels, tastes, smells, and sounds.

For additional practice, turn to pages 135–136.

GRAMMAR

SIZE, SHAPE, COLOR

Some describing words tell about size, shape, or color.

I have a <u>little</u> snake.

It wears a <u>round</u> hat.

The hat is <u>purple</u>.

NUMBER

Some describing words tell <u>how many</u>.

There are <u>ten</u> dots on the hat.

Exercises

A. Add a describing word to each sentence.

1. I keep my snake in a _____ box.
2. He has escaped _____ times.
3. He hides under our _____ table.

B. Read each sentence. Write the describing word that tells about each underlined noun.

1. My snakes can spell seven <u>words</u>.
2. They make letters with their little <u>bodies</u>.
3. One <u>snake</u> crawled away from me.
4. I put the snakes on a square <u>blanket</u>.
5. My snakes won blue <u>ribbons</u>.
6. Wow, look at that huge <u>snake</u>!

For additional practice, turn to pages 135–136.

Describing Words That Compare

ER

A describing word that ends with er compares two things.

The brachiosaurus had a longer neck than the ornithomimus.

EST

A describing word that ends with est compares more than two things.

The plateosaurus had the longest neck of the three.

Exercises

Choose the correct describing word in each sentence.

1. My dinosaur book is (longer, longest) than yours.

2. Which dinosaur was the (faster, fastest) runner of all?

For additional practice, turn to page 137.

Kids on Language

My name is Jason Lucki. Last summer I visited my grandmother in Germany. My grandmother can speak German and English. In Germany the signs aren't written in English. They're written in German, of course! I could read the signs that had pictures on them, like a bus for the bus stop or silverware for a place to eat. Some German words sound a lot like English. Ja means "yes." The word for "cat" is Katze. In German you say Auto instead of "car" and Haus when you mean "house."

NOW

An **action verb** is a word that tells what someone or something does. A verb can tell about an action that happens now. Add s to an action verb that tells what one person, animal, or thing does.

> **Two boys dig for fossils.**
>
> **A girl digs for fossils, too.**

Exercises

A. Choose the correct verb in each sentence.

1. Scientists (dig, digs) in the ground for dinosaur fossils.
2. One scientist (find, finds) a bone.
3. Another one (discover, discovers) a tooth.
4. Scientists (work, works) carefully.
5. This bone (look, looks) VERY big!

B. Use a word from the box to finish each sentence. Add _s_ to the verb if you need to. Write the sentences.

run bite roar stop see

1. One dinosaur _____ another one far away.

2. They _____ fast.

3. One _____ the other's foot.

4. That dinosaur _____.

5. Then it _____ and stands still.

For additional practice, turn to page 138.

GRAMMAR

PAST

A verb can tell about an action that happened in the past. Many verbs end with <u>ed</u> to tell about something that happened in the past.

We <u>called</u> Grandma on the phone.

We <u>talked</u> for a long time.

Exercises

A. Make each sentence tell about the past. Choose the correct verb.

1. We (asks, asked) Grandma to visit.
2. She (kiss, kissed) us hello.
3. Grandma (jumps, jumped) rope with us.
4. Everyone (laugh, laughed) at her jokes.
5. She (helps, helped) us clean our rooms.

B. Complete each sentence by adding a verb from the box. Make the verb tell about the past. Write the sentence.

lick	**enjoy**	**help**	**play**

1. Grandma ———— board games with us.
2. She ———— us make a cake.
3. We even ———— the spoons.
4. We ———— Grandma's visit.

For additional practice, turn to page 139.

IS, AM, ARE

Some verbs do not show action. They tell what someone or something is like.

The verbs is, am, and are tell about now.

My sister is quiet.

I am noisy.

My sister and I are friends.

Exercise

Choose the correct verb in each sentence.

1. Lunch (am, is) ready.
2. The hamburgers (is, are) hot.
3. The milk (is, am) cold.
4. I (am, is) thirsty.
5. My family (is, are) hungry.

For additional practice, turn to page 140.

Was, Were

WAS, WERE

The verbs <u>was</u> and <u>were</u> tell about the past.

I <u>was</u> foolish.

My friends <u>were</u> careless.

Exercise

Choose the correct verb in each sentence.

1. We (was, were) inside.
2. Our bikes (was, were) outside.
3. We (was, were) too tired to put them in the garage.
4. The next morning I (was, were) very sad.
5. My new bike (was, were) not there.

For additional practice, turn to page 141.

GRAMMAR

Has, Have, Had

HAS, HAVE

The verbs has and have tell about now.

> **Mr. Brown has a big yard.**
>
> **Holly and Peter have rakes.**

HAD

The verb had tells about the past.

> **Last fall we had more leaves to rake.**

Exercise

Choose the correct verb in each sentence.

1. Our neighbor (have, has) an apple tree.
2. Last year the tree (has, had) lots of apples.
3. This year it (had, has) fewer apples.
4. We (has, have) fun picking up apples.
5. Holly (has, have) a pail for the apples.

For additional practice, turn to page 142.

Helping Verbs

HELPING VERBS

A **helping verb** works with the main verb to show action.

Use <u>has</u>, <u>have</u>, and <u>had</u> with other verbs to show action that happened in the past.

> **Steve <u>has</u> worked hard.**
>
> **Ellen and Katie <u>have</u> helped.**
>
> **They <u>had</u> stopped earlier for a snack.**

Exercise

Choose the correct helping verb in each sentence.

1. We (has, have) built a new playground.
2. Mom and Dad (had, has) sawed the boards before.
3. Donna (has, have) sanded the wood.
4. They (has, have) painted the fence.

For additional practice, turn to page 143.

See and Give

SEE, GIVE

The verbs see and give tell about now. Add s to tell what one person, animal, or thing does.

The children see their teacher.

Ms. Simms sees that her children are tired.

Luis gives the puppets to the teacher.

Two helpers give her the storybook.

SAW, GAVE

The verbs saw and gave tell about the past. These action verbs do not add ed to tell about the past.

We saw the teacher yesterday.

Shanda gave me one puppet.

Exercises

A. Choose the correct verb for each sentence.

1. My mom (give, gives) a talk about her job.
2. My classmates (see, sees) her tools.
3. Mom (see, sees) sick animals where she works.
4. She (give, gives) them shots once a year.
5. Her helpers (give, gives) the pets baths.

B. Change the verb to make each sentence tell about the past. Write the sentences.

1. The children see the man with the cook's hat.
2. Mr. Lee gives them directions for a Chinese dish.
3. They see a very big pan.
4. Amy sees Mr. Lee chop the food fast.

For additional practice, turn to page 144.

COME, RUN

The verbs come and run tell about now. Add s to tell what one person, animal, or thing does.

We come to help.
Sara comes to help.

We run in the yard.
A dog runs in the yard.

CAME, RAN

The verbs came and ran tell about the past.

Last week we came to visit.
The dog ran around the tree.

Exercises

A. Choose the correct verb in each sentence.

1. Two girls (come, comes) to help outside.
2. Mom (come, comes) to wash the windows.
3. Sara (come, comes) to help in the garden.
4. The dog (runs, run) away from me.

B. Change the verb to make each sentence tell about the past. Write the sentences.

1. The dog comes after the ball.
2. It runs away with the ball.
3. She runs next to the dog.

For additional practice, turn to page 145.

Go and Do

GO, DO

The verbs go and do tell about now. Add es to tell what one person, animal, or thing does.

Bees go to the hive.

A bee goes to the hive.

They do hard work.

The bee does hard work.

WENT, DID

To tell about the past, the spelling of these verbs changes to went and did.

Yesterday the bees went to find flowers.

They did a lot of flying.

94

GRAMMAR

Exercises

A. Choose the correct verb in each sentence.

1. Dr. Medina (go, goes) to school to study bees.
2. Worker bees (go, goes) to find flowers.
3. A bee (do, does) a dance to tell others where the flowers are.
4. Each bee (do, does) its share of the work.

B. Change the verb to make each sentence tell about the past. Write the sentences.

1. One bee goes inside the hive.
2. Soon all the bees go inside.
3. Each worker bee does its own job.
4. The queen bee does the most important job of all.

For additional practice, turn to page 146.

AGREEMENT

When the naming part of a sentence tells about one, add <u>s</u> to the verb.

A sea turtle <u>grows</u> very large.

When a naming part tells about more than one, the verb does not end in <u>s</u>.

Sea turtles <u>swim</u> a long way.

Exercises

A. Choose the correct verb in each sentence.

1. Sea turtles (return, returns) to the beach.
2. They (swim, swims) many miles in the ocean.
3. A mother turtle (crawl, crawls) up the sandy beach.
4. It (dig, digs) a nest in the sand.
5. It (lay, lays) eggs in the nest.

B. Write a word from the box to finish each sentence. Add <u>s</u> to the verb if you need to.

dive climb help know swim

1. Baby turtles _____ out of their sandy nest.
2. The babies _____ that they must go to the sea.
3. Often a hungry gull _____ down.
4. Sometimes people _____ the babies.
5. Then the baby turtles _____ in the water.

For additional practice, turn to page 147.

GRAMMAR

CONTRACTIONS

A **contraction** is a short way to write two words.

When a contraction is made, one or more letters are left out. An **apostrophe** (') takes the place of the missing letter or letters.

> **The octopus <u>did not</u> catch a fish.**
> **The octopus <u>didn't</u> catch a fish.**

Exercises

A. Read each sentence. Change the underlined words to a contraction.

1. The giant clam <u>was not</u> small.
2. <u>It is</u> bigger than my head!
3. Some starfish <u>do not</u> have five arms.
4. Sea horses <u>are not</u> fast swimmers.
5. <u>They are</u> fun to watch.

B. Read each sentence. Write the words that make up the underlined contraction.

1. I've seen a show about coral reefs.
2. Animals in a coral reef aren't able to live in dirty water.
3. It's hard for them to eat and breathe.
4. Saving a coral reef isn't easy.
5. Coral reefs didn't grow quickly.

For additional practice, turn to page 148.

Troublesome Words

TO, TOO, TWO

The words to, too, and two sound the same, but they have different meanings.

Use to when you mean "in the direction of."

The crabs walked to the empty shells.

Use too when you mean "also."

The crabs rested, too.

Use two when you mean "one more than one."

The two crabs needed bigger shells.

Exercise

Complete each sentence with to, too, or two.

1. A hermit crab has _____ claws.

2. Sometimes the crab grows larger than its shell, _____.

3. Then it goes _____ a new home.

For additional practice, turn to page 149.

THERE, THEIR, THEY'RE

The words there, their, and they're sound the same, but they have different meanings.

Use there when you mean "in that place."

Alligators live there.

Use their when you mean "belonging to them."

The water is their home.

Use they're when you mean "they are."

They're floating on the water.

Exercise

Choose the correct word to complete each sentence.

1. Alligators spend most of (they're, their) time in the water.
2. They catch most of their food (there, they're).
3. (Their, They're) good swimmers.

For additional practice, turn to page 150.

FAMILY STORIES

My name is Shanaz Biggs. My grandfather grew up in Guatemala. He spoke mostly Spanish. My mother says that he loved to tell stories. When she was a little girl in Jamaica, storytelling was one way families had fun together. I like to tell stories, too, but I tell them in English. Every year at Kwanzaa people in my family take turns telling stories.

Handwriting

A B C D E F G

H I J K L M N

O P Q R S T

U V W X Y Z

A B C D E F G

H I J K L M N

O P Q R S T

U V W X Y Z

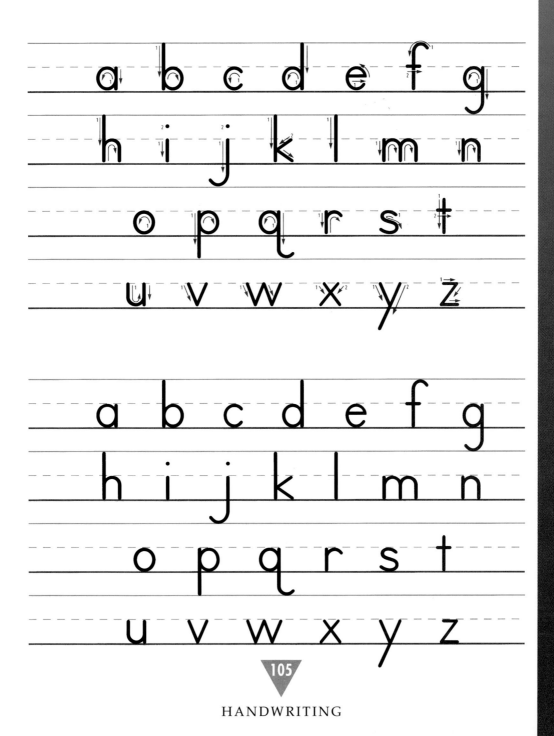

A B C D E F G
H I J K L M N
O P Q R S T
U V W X Y Z

A B C D E F G
H I J K L M N
O P Q R S T
U V W X Y Z

106

Lowercase Cursive Alphabet

a b c d e f g
h i j k l m n
o p q r s t
u v w x y z

a b c d e f g
h i j k l m n
o p q r s t
u v w x y z

107

HANDWRITING

Shape

Do not put loops in these letters or leave spaces.
Make retrace strokes smooth.

correct

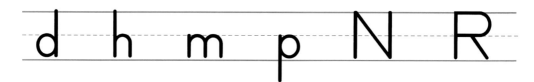

incorrect

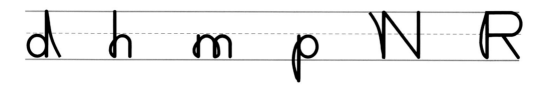

Close circle letters. Connect lines.

correct

incorrect

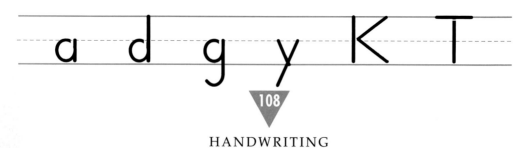

HANDWRITING

Spacing Letters

Letters should not be written too close together or too far apart.

just right   **too close**   **too far apart**

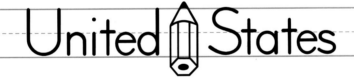

Spacing Words

The space between words should be as wide as a pencil.

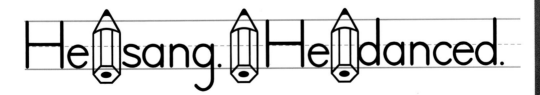

Spacing Sentences

Leave a pencil space between sentences.

109

HANDWRITING

Position

Write all letters so that they sit on the bottom line.

incorrect   **correct**

John   John

Size

Write tall letters to touch the top line.
Write tail letters to touch the descender line.
Write short letters to touch the midline.

incorrect   **correct**

Monday   Monday

Stroke

Make your letters smooth and even.
They should not be too light or too dark.

too light   **too dark**   **smooth and even**

mop   **mop**   mop

incorrect **correct**

t   t   Cross at the midline.
The **t** could look like **T**.

incorrect **correct**

h   b   Circle to the stem.
The **b** could look like **h**.

incorrect **correct**

h   n   Start at the midline.
The **n** could look like **h**.

incorrect **correct**

q   p   Circle to the right.
The **p** could look like
g or **q**.

incorrect **correct**

u   a   Start slightly below
the midline and circle
to the left, touching
the midline.
The **a** could look like **u**.

111

HANDWRITING

incorrect   **correct**

q   g

Curve the tail stroke on **g** to the left.
The **g** could look like **q**.

incorrect   **correct**

q   q

Curve the tail stroke on **q** to the right.
The **q** could look like **g**.

incorrect   **correct**

v   u

Retrace the bottom line.
The **u** could look like **v**.

incorrect   **correct**

Σ   z

Go straight across to the right.
The **z** could look like **s**.

incorrect   **correct**

Y   y

Start at the midline.
The **y** could look like uppercase **Y**.

Common Errors — Manuscript Letters

incorrect **correct**

Use strokes that go straight across. The **I** could look like lowercase **l**.

incorrect **correct**

Use strokes that go straight down. The **H** could look like **A**.

incorrect **correct**

Close the circle. The **O** could look like **C**.

incorrect **correct**

Use a stroke that goes straight across. The **G** could look like uppercase **C**.

incorrect **correct**

Circle to the right and close. The **B** could look like **R**.

HANDWRITING

incorrect   **correct**

Do not loop **i**.
The **i** could look like **e**.

incorrect   **correct**

Touch the top line.
The **l** could look like **e**.

incorrect   **correct**

Be sure the slant stroke
returns to the bottom line.
The **u** could look like **v**.

incorrect   **correct**

Loop left.
The **g** could look like **q**.

SENTENCES

Read each group of words. Write <u>yes</u> if the words make a sentence. Write <u>no</u> if the words do not make a sentence.

Example:

I like to play soccer.

yes

1. practice on Saturdays

2. lost the first game

3. My sister helps me.

4. We practice every day.

5. made a goal

6. my sister and I

7. I thank my sister.

8. Pete is our best player.

9. Teresa and Gillian

10. My dad comes to our games.

Write each sentence. Underline the naming part.

Example:

The dogs like music.

1. **The school has a band.**
2. **Rover leads the band.**
3. **The flutes are the softest.**
4. **Jack plays the trumpet.**
5. **His friend plays the tuba.**
6. **They practice every day.**
7. **Pepe is the smallest dog of all.**
8. **The band marches outside.**
9. **Fido leads the other dogs.**
10. **The parade begins at noon.**

Additional Practice

JOINING NAMING PARTS

Complete the sentences by joining the naming parts.
Write the sentences.

Example:

Michael cut the grass.

Mary cut the grass.

Michael and Mary cut the grass.

1. **Eli made the beds.**
   Miguel made the beds.
   _____ and _____ **made the beds.**

2. **Tony made sandwiches.**
   Jan made sandwiches.
   _____ and _____ **made sandwiches.**

3. **Patty poured milk.**
   Tessa poured milk.
   _____ and _____ **poured milk.**

4. **Dan washed the dog.**
   Cindy washed the dog.
   _____ and _____ **washed the dog.**

Write each sentence. Underline the telling part.

Example:

We <u>return bottles to the store.</u>

1. **Friends help us.**
2. **Molly saves plastic containers.**
3. **The newspapers are in boxes.**
4. **Frank collects aluminum cans.**
5. **The neighbors give us glass bottles.**
6. **We sort the trash.**
7. **Mom drives to the recycling center.**
8. **We dump trash into bins.**

Additional Practice

Join the telling parts of each pair of sentences.
Use the word <u>and</u>. Write new sentences.

Example:

Keena adds.

Keena subtracts.

Keena adds and subtracts.

1. **Seth reads.**
   Seth writes.

2. **Brian listens to his teacher.**
   Brian does his homework.

3. **Amy prints spelling words.**
   Amy checks her paper.

4. **Mike writes a story.**
   Mike draws pictures.

5. **Maria raises her hand.**
   Maria tells the answer.

WORD ORDER

Write each group of words in the correct order.

Example:

plays Reba tennis.

Reba plays tennis.

1. **to be wants She a star.**
2. **Reba day practices every.**
3. **she wins Sometimes games.**
4. **games Sometimes loses she.**
5. **with other children plays tennis Reba.**
6. **better is getting Reba.**
7. **started Nate tennis lessons.**
8. **fast run He can.**

STATEMENTS

Read each statement. Find the statements that have mistakes. Write those statements correctly.

Example:

ben is my friend

Ben is my friend.

1. he uses a wheelchair
2. at school Ben is in my class
3. we study together
4. Mom takes us to the movies.
5. sometimes Ben needs my help
6. then I open doors for him
7. Ben has a lot of stamps.
8. we like to trade stamps.

Write each sentence correctly.

Example:

what is your penguin's name

What is your penguin's name?

1. my penguin's name is Tuffy

2. where did you get her

3. does your baby brother like her

4. can he play with Tuffy

5. I pretend Tuffy is real

6. would you like to hear her talk

7. why are penguins mostly black and white

8. is Tuffy a stuffed animal

9. when can I hold her

10. my mom loves penguins

Additional Practice

Read each sentence. Is it an exclamation or a command? Write the sentences correctly.

Example:

Stay near shore

Stay near shore.

1. Bring your bathing suit
2. Hooray, we're going to the beach
3. Invite a friend
4. We'll have lots of fun
5. I'm so hot
6. Jump into the water
7. Don't splash
8. Here come the waves
9. Wow, there's a shark
10. What an adventure

END MARKS

Write each sentence correctly. Add a period, a question mark, or an exclamation point.

Example:

Lee is my good friend

Lee is my good friend.

1. **Do you know why I like him**
2. **He shares his toys with me**
3. **He tells me funny jokes**
4. **How he makes me laugh**
5. **What fun we have together**
6. **Do you have a special friend**
7. **Tell me your friend's name**
8. **Is his name Tom**

NOUNS

Read each sentence. Write the noun or nouns. For each noun, tell if it names a person, an animal, a place, or a thing.

Example:

These friends help in their neighborhood.

friends—people

neighborhood—place

1. Some children work in a garden.
2. The man shows what to do.
3. A girl plants corn.
4. She uses a shovel and a hoe.
5. A boy waters the daisies.
6. Even the squirrel helps!
7. It picks up nuts from the ground.
8. Then it runs up the tree.

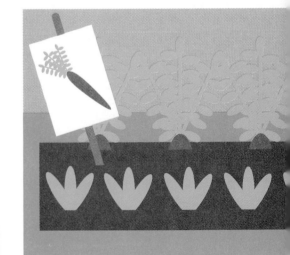

Write each sentence correctly. Add capital letters and periods where they are needed.

Example:

mr davis has an orange tree in his yard.

Mr. Davis has an orange tree in his yard.

1. **Look, mrs sanchez has a watering can.**
2. **What did alexandra bring?**
3. **Yes, dr roberts brought a shovel.**
4. **He and mrs grove brought the tree.**
5. **We can plant it in ms handy's yard.**
6. **Then jennifer will have fresh oranges.**

Additional Practice

A. Choose the correct word to complete each sentence. Write the sentences.

Example:

Our fish is named (goldy, Goldy).

Our fish is named <u>Goldy</u>.

1. **We went to (san francisco, San Francisco).**
2. **It is in (california, California).**
3. **We brought our cat, (sandy, Sandy).**

B. Write each sentence correctly. Add capital letters where they are needed.

Example:

My dog, frisky, came from seattle.

My dog, Frisky, came from Seattle.

1. **Our dog, peke, is very cute.**
2. **He comes from the city of peking.**
3. **It is a city in china.**

A. Read each sentence. Write the name of the day, month, or holiday that is written correctly.

Example:

Our county fair is held in (august, August).

August

1. Each year, we go on a field trip in (April, april).

2. On (tuesday, Tuesday), we went to a farm.

3. We bought seeds for (may, May) flowers.

4. I planted my seeds on (wednesday, Wednesday).

5. I gave the plant to my mother on (Mother's Day, mother's day).

6. In (June, june) the plant had big flowers.

7. They were in bloom on the (fourth of july, Fourth of July).

8. I took my flowers to the county fair in (August, august).

B. Write each sentence correctly. Add capital letters where they are needed.

Example:

It snowed on new year's day.

It snowed on New Year's Day.

1. **On monday, Mr. Quinn yelled at the dog.**

2. **On tuesday, he slammed his door.**

3. **He was grouchy all through january.**

4. **On valentine's day, he got three valentines.**

5. **He started smiling more in february.**

6. **He wore a tall hat on presidents' day.**

7. **He laughed out loud in march.**

8. **He won a blue ribbon in july.**

A. Write each sentence correctly. Add capital letters where they are needed.

Example:

Have you read henry and mudge?

Have you read Henry and Mudge?

1. I liked reading the stinky cheese man.

2. Another funny book is old turtle's baseball stories.

3. If you like baseball, you'll like frank and ernest play ball.

B. Write these book titles correctly.

Example:

time of wonder

Time of Wonder

chicken soup and rice

the bicycle man

peter and the wolf

Additional Practice

PLURAL NOUNS

A. Choose the correct noun in each sentence. Write the noun.

Example:

Our two (friend, friends) are getting ready for the carnival.

friends

1. The carnival begins with a parade of many (clown, clowns).

2. The first clown is riding on an (elephant, elephants).

3. Some (child, children) are in the parade.

4. They are carrying (pets, pet).

5. Two baby (fox, foxes) are in a cage.

6. Some (men, man) are riding horses.

B. Make each underlined noun mean more than one. Write the sentences.

Example:

I have been to two <u>circus</u>.
I have been to two <u>circuses</u>.

1. **The circus has many <u>clown</u>.**
2. **Most clowns have big <u>foot</u>.**
3. **Many <u>dog</u> do tricks.**
4. **Big dogs come out of little <u>box</u>.**
5. **The lion tamer has many <u>lion</u>.**
6. **Three <u>man</u> are jugglers.**
7. **Two <u>woman</u> ride horses bareback.**
8. **All the <u>tiger</u> come out last.**

PRACTICE

PRONOUNS

A. Write the pronoun that can take the place of the underlined word or words.

Example:

<u>The animals</u> watch.   He She It They   **They**

1. <u>Mom</u> was sleeping.	He	She	It	They
2. <u>Dad</u> was in the boat.	He	She	It	They
3. <u>An owl</u> hoots.	He	She	It	They
4. <u>Two mice</u> run by.	He	She	It	They
5. <u>Sam and Esme</u> yell.	He	She	It	They

B. Read each sentence. Think of a pronoun for the underlined word or words. Write the new sentence.

Example:

<u>Ari</u> likes to go camping.

He likes to go camping.

1. <u>Sara</u> built a campfire.

2. <u>James</u> told a story.

3. <u>The story</u> was scary.

A. Look at the picture. Then write each sentence. Circle the describing word. Draw a line under the noun it tells about.

Example:

There are (five) <u>snakes</u> in the parade.

1. **They wear tiny hats.**
2. **Meg's hat has a square shape.**
3. **Max has a yellow belly.**
4. **Sal has a round balloon.**
5. **Fred blows a loud horn.**

B. Look at the picture on page 135. Use words from the box to complete each sentence. Write the sentence.

little	bumpy	smooth
square	sweet	hissing

Example:

Sam is holding a _____ sign.

Sam is holding a <u>square</u> sign.

1. **Meg is pulling some _____ bells.**

2. **The _____ ground makes the bells jingle.**

3. **The apple tastes _____ .**

4. **The snakes make _____ sounds.**

5. **They all have _____ skin.**

Choose the correct describing word. Write the sentences.

Example:

Some dinosaurs were (strong, stronger) than others.

Some dinosaurs were <u>stronger</u> than others.

1. Some had (sharper, sharpest) teeth than others.

2. The Brachiosaurus was one of the (large, largest) dinosaurs of all.

3. It was (taller, tallest) than 40 feet.

4. Its front legs were (longer, longest) than its back ones.

5. It could reach the (higher, highest) leaves.

137

PRACTICE

Additional Practice

Choose a verb from the box to complete each sentence. Add s to the verb if you need to. Write the sentence.

enjoy	tell	like
help	paint	sew
work	sing	read

Example:

My class _____ to put on plays.

My class likes to put on plays.

1. **Each child _____ with the work.**

2. **Some people _____ the costumes.**

3. **Others _____ the background.**

4. **We all _____ very hard.**

5. **Our play _____ about dinosaurs.**

6. **We _____ working together.**

7. **Ms. Arnold _____ our lines with us.**

Find the verb in each sentence. Make it tell about the past. Then write the new sentence.

Example:

My family visits the zoo.

My family <u>visited</u> the zoo.

1. **We watch the animals.**
2. **The monkeys climb ropes.**
3. **The seals jump off rocks.**
4. **My sister wants to buy a balloon.**
5. **Later, we munch on popcorn.**
6. **Two apes play with a tire.**
7. **Dad talks to a parrot!**
8. **We laugh all the way home.**

IS, AM, ARE

Choose is, am, or are to finish each sentence.
Then write the sentence.

Example:

The state fair _____ fun.

The state fair is fun.

1. **The clowns _____ silly.**

2. **That cowgirl _____ brave.**

3. **I _____ so excited!**

4. **Some animals _____ loud.**

5. **My brother _____ excited, too.**

6. **Dad's apple pie _____ yummy!**

7. **I _____ thrilled to be at the fair.**

8. **Rosa's pet pig _____ a winner.**

Choose <u>was</u> or <u>were</u> to finish each sentence.
Then write the sentence.

Example:

J. Mouse _____ happy.

J. Mouse <u>was</u> happy.

1. **Two presents _____ on the table.**

2. **One gift _____ pretty.**

3. **The other one _____ ugly.**

4. **Both boxes _____ big.**

5. **The mouse's eyes _____ big.**

6. **J. Mouse _____ sad.**

7. **The box _____ empty!**

8. **The two mice _____ good friends.**

HAS, HAVE, HAD

Choose has, have, or had to finish each sentence. Then write the sentence.

Example:

Last year, the boys _____ a contest.

Last year, the boys had a contest.

1. **This year, the girls and boys _____ another contest.**

2. **The children _____ board games to play.**

3. **Monica and Darrell _____ a checkers set.**

4. **Today Mr. Wills _____ dominoes.**

5. **Last year, two boys _____ a prize for the winner.**

6. **Yesterday, one girl _____ an idea for a new prize.**

7. **Today Mr. Wills _____ a big blue ribbon.**

8. **Now all the children _____ fun playing board games.**

Write each sentence. Circle the helping verb.

Example:

We (had) left home early.

1. Now we have arrived at the camp.

2. Tom and Bill have unloaded the car.

3. Mr. Green had shopped for food the day before.

4. Bob has gathered firewood.

5. Something strange has happened.

6. A spaceship has landed nearby!

Additional Practice

SEE AND GIVE

Read each sentence. Make the underlined verb tell about the past. Write the sentence.

Example:

Shayla <u>sees</u> a picture in a cookbook.

Shayla <u>saw</u> a picture in a cookbook.

1. She <u>sees</u> a recipe, too.

2. She <u>gives</u> the book to her mother.

3. The recipe <u>gives</u> a list of things needed.

4. Shayla's mother <u>gives</u> her some help.

5. Later, Kim <u>sees</u> huge cookies.

6. Shayla <u>gives</u> her a monster cookie.

A. Choose the correct verb. Write the sentence.

Example:

We (come, comes) to the park to work.

We come to the park to work.

1. **The families (come, comes) to help clean up the park.**
2. **She (come, comes) to pick up litter.**
3. **Dad (come, comes) to paint.**
4. **My dog (runs, run) after the bird.**
5. **Two birds (run, runs) away.**

B. Change the verb in each sentence above so that it tells about the past. Write the sentence.

Example:

We come to the park to work.

We came to the park to work.

Additional Practice

A. Read each sentence. Write the correct verb.

Example:

The wasps _____ their work.   do   does

do

1. **The wasps _____ to their nest under the roof.**   go   goes

2. **They _____ many things.**   do   does

3. **One wasp _____ the hardest job.**   do   does

4. **Other wasps _____ for food.**   go   goes

B. Change the verb in each sentence above so that it tells about the past. Write the sentence.

Example:

The wasps do their work.

The wasps did their work.

AGREEMENT

Choose the correct verb. Write the sentence.

Example:

Sea otters (live, lives) in the ocean.

Sea otters live in the ocean.

1. **They (eats, eat) crabs and shellfish.**

2. **A sea otter hardly ever (comes, come) to the shore.**

3. **It even (sleep, sleeps) on the water.**

4. **Sea otters (need, needs) their fur.**

5. **Sometimes sticky oil (cover, covers) an otter's fur.**

6. **Some people (cleans, clean) the oil from the fur.**

7. **Ships (spill, spills) oil into the ocean.**

Additional Practice

CONTRACTIONS

A. Read each sentence. Write the contraction for the two words in parentheses ( ).

Example:

Some pandas (do not) look like bears.

don't

1. **People (did not) want the pandas to die.**

2. **Pandas (are not) easy to keep in zoos.**

3. **Giant pandas (do not) live without bamboo to eat.**

4. **Saving pandas (is not) easy.**

B. Read each sentence. Write the two words that make up the underlined contraction.

Example:

The zoo <u>wasn't</u> crowded.

was not

1. **I <u>didn't</u> see the zoo's panda.**

2. **The shy panda <u>isn't</u> outside.**

TO, TOO, TWO

A. Write the correct word for each sentence.

Example:

A honey guide flew (too, to) a branch.

to

1. **A honey guide and a ratel are (to, two) animal partners.**
2. **The honey guide flies (to, two) a bees' nest but can't open it.**
3. **It looks (to, too) the ratel for help.**

B. Complete each sentence with to, too, or two. Write the sentences.

Example:

The _____ animals help each other.

The two animals help each other.

1. **The ratel goes _____ the nest.**
2. **The honey guide eats from the nest, _____.**
3. **The _____ animals have a sweet friendship.**

Additional Practice

THERE, THEIR, THEY'RE

Read each sentence. Write the correct word.

Example:

Elephants grow for most
of (there, their) lives.

their

1. Many elephants make (their, there) homes in Africa.

2. (They're, There) the largest land animals.

3. Young elephants live with (their, there) mothers.

4. (There, They're) watched over by the whole herd.

5. Hunters kill elephants for (their, there) ivory tusks.

6. Elephants (they're, there) may be in danger.

7. Some countries (they're, there) have passed laws.

8. (Their, They're) trying to save the elephants.

Joining telling parts of sentences,
44–45, 120
Journal, 4

Letters
friendly, 12–13

Mechanics
apostrophe, 98–99, 148
comma
addresses, dates, greetings,
closings, 12–13
exclamation point, 52–53, 54–55,
124–125
period, 48–49, 52–53, 54–55, 122,
124, 125
question mark, 50–51, 54–55, 123, 125
Multicultural perspectives, 75, 81, 102

Naming part of sentence, 38–39, 117
joining naming parts, 40–41, 118
Nouns
definition of, 56
people, animals, places, things,
56–57, 126
plural, 68–69, 70–71, 72–73, 132–133
proper
names of days and months,
62–63, 129–130
names of holidays, 64–65,
129–130
names of special animals and
places, 60–61, 128
special names of people, 58–59,
127
titles of books, 66–67, 131
titles of people, 58–59, 127

Paragraph, 5
descriptive, 18–19
how-to, 28–29
of information, 22–23
Persuasive poster, 32–33
Play, 26–27
Poem, 20–21
Pronouns
I, he, she, it, they, 74, 134
Proofreading, 2–3
Publishing, 2–3

Question. *See* **Sentences.**

Research report, 30–31
Responding and revising, 2–3

See and *give,* 90–91, 144
Sentences
about pictures, 10–11
command, 52–53, 124
definition of, 10, 36
detail sentences, 5, 19, 22–23

exclamation, 52–53, 124
joining naming parts, 40–41, 118
joining telling parts, 44–45, 120
kinds of, 48–49, 50–51, 52–53, 122,
    123, 124
parts of, 38–39, 42–43, 117, 119
punctuation of, 48–49, 50–51, 52–53,
    54–55, 122–125
question, 50–51, 123
statement, 48–49, 122
topic sentence, 5, 18–19, 22–23
word order in, 46–47, 121
Statement. *See* **Sentences.**
Story, 8–9
    personal, 6–7
Superlatives, 80, 137

Telling part of sentence, 42–43, 119
    joining telling parts, 44–45, 120
Tenses, 82–83, 84–85, 138, 139
Test, writing for a, 34
Thank-you note, 16
There, their, they're, 101, 150
Time-order words, 6–7, 28
Titles
    of books, 66–67, 131
    of people, 58–59, 127
To, too, two, 100, 149
Topic sentence, 5, 18–19, 22–23
Troublesome words
    there, their, they're, 101, 150
    to, too, two, 100, 149

Verbs
    action verbs, 82–83, 84–85, 138, 139
    agreement, 96–97, 147
    helping verbs, 89, 143
    come and *run,* 92–93, 145
    go and *do,* 94–95, 146
    has, have, had, 88, 89, 142, 143
    is, am, are, 86, 140
    see and *give,* 90–91, 144
    that do not show action, 86, 87, 88,
        140, 141, 142
    that tell about now, 82–83, 138
    that tell about the past, 84–85, 139
    was and *were,* 87, 141

Was and *were,* 87, 141
Word order. *See* **Sentences.**
Writing
    book report, 24–25
    descriptive paragraph, 18–19
    envelope, 17
    friendly letter, 12–13
    how-to paragraph, 28–29
    informational paragraph, 22–23
    invitation, 14–15
    journal, 4
    paragraph, 5
    personal story, 6–7
    persuasive poster, 32–33
    play, 26–27
    poem, 20–21
    research report, 30–31
    sentences about a picture, 10–11
    story, 8–9
    thank-you note, 16
    writing for a test, 34
    writing process, 2–3

Usage. *See* **Verbs.**